December 10, 2014

In one of the Scandinavian countries (I don't remember which one because they all seem the same to me) the police killed someone for the 1st time in the country's history (founded in 1944). The police apologized and the entire country mourned. That's not a reflection of the police or the person who died (he had mental issues), but a reflection of the larger society. In that country the police don't carry weapons, but neither does anyone else.

Now go to America.

Just as Black people aren't the reason for justice inequality and racism, police aren't either. It's the larger society (us) who are the problem for not having different priorities. It's true that far too many American police officers are far too violent, and White privilege exists, and justice inequality exists, but the police didn't create any of that. On top of the racism and income inequality, we live in an extremely violent society that worships guns.

"We won't limit any part of the problem with laws and policies that make sense. And we certainly wont be bothered to elect people to represent the policies and laws we want. But we "will" ask cops to protect us from all the violence we allow and all those violent people violence creates. Let the cops do the dirty work and deal with it. And God love 'em for doing it. Better them than us. All cops are trained in street safety: How to protect themselves at all times from "potential" dangers from those dangerous streets we ask them to patrol. Part of that street safety is taking control of every situation. Being suspicious of every person they come in contact with. Staying alive is an important part of their job. Is that part of your job? Put yourself in their shoes. How would you react to someone who doesn't tell you his name? It's a simple question. "What's your name?" Would you be suspicious? If you were trained in street safety would that raise a red flag? Bad guys lie. They may say they are picking up their kids, or say they're going to faint, or say they don't have any weapons on them. Cops hear it all, and they hear it all the time because they're usually dealing with bad guys. And bad guys evade simple questions.

So, how do good cops determine if they are talking to a bad guy who is lying or a good guy who is telling the truth? After all, if someone calls 911 about a suspicious person, the police have to respond. When they arrive on the scene, they then ask this guy a simple question. "What's your name?" But he refuses to give it to them. They are the people we've asked to protect us from bad guys and he didn't answer a simple question. Only bad guys don't answer simple questions like that. We've given cops the authority to ask any of us simple questions when they are responding to a call and this guy's doing what bad guys do, he's avoiding a simple question. Warning bells go off. However, let's stop there and see the situation from the guy's point if view. He's black. He's been accused of doing bad things all his life because he's black. Non-blacks have treated him with suspicion all his life because they think all blacks are guilty of something. They follow him around stores, they don't wait on him right way in restaurants, they ignore him at the car dealership. He's been good all his life and he's always being treated like he's doing something bad. And every time it happens he's a little less invested in the community that consistently treats him like a criminal. It's exhausting and he's tired of it.

So he sits on a bench, waiting for his kid, minding his own business, out of the snow in a breezeway, just beside a jewelry store (I made up that last part). Some bigot calls 911 that a suspicious guy (black) is casing the jewelry store. 911 gets a description (black male) and dispatches the cops. The bigot doesn't tell 911: "Oh by the way, I'm a bigot and only think this guy is suspicious because he's Black," but part of the call is a description, which includes the man's skin color.

A normal, non-bigoted cop responds, having returned from a police funeral the previous week because a fellow cop had been shot and killed during a routine traffic stop, which heightens her street safety (I made up that last part).

In that lily-white town, they see the only black guy around, minding his own business, and the cop asks his name. A simple question. And this guy knows, he just "knows" someone called the cops because he's black. He knows because it's happened before. The previous time, the cop was a dick and called him a nigger and handcuffed him for no legitimate reason. It taught him that you couldn't trust cops. So when this cop asks him his name, that man feels he is being harassed, just because he's black, and he can't take it anymore. He decides to take a stand, and won't answer what seems like a simple question. The man instead insists, in a very nice (con-artist) way why she's asking. But she's a cop. Cops don't answer questions they ask the questions. We, society didn't give this guy authority to ask any questions.

The cop, who we have trained to protect us from violent people and who we have given authority to ask these questions, gets suspicious. She calls for backup. The next cop was talking to the guy earlier. The Black guys thinks they're buds. But they aren't buds. The guy is friendly with the 2nd cop but the cop isn't friendly back. He's barking orders, getting angry. Kind of acting like a dick. Not listening. Getting aggressive. Keeps asking the guy's name, but the guy doesn't give it because that's not what's important to him now. Getting his kid is what's important. But the cops can't get a simple answer out of this guy and their street safety kicks in. What's his problem? What's he trying to hide? We'd better be careful with this guy. Who knows what he's going to do next. He could have a weapon on him. Look. He's yelling about a kid instead of just answering our simple question. What's wrong with him? Who does that? Something must be wrong with him. 5150? Are we in danger? Are others in danger? Oh no. See that kid nearby? Is "he" in danger? It's all escalating so fast. We'd better subdue him quickly and get control of the situation because that's what the people expect us to do. How would you have reacted if you were the cops?

Someone takes a video and posts it. News outlets show it. People react. But no one takes responsibility for the society they, themselves (we) have created. Some blame the black guy for not cooperating. Some blame the police for excessive force. But neither are to blame. Can you guess who is?" -Patricia Wright

"I consider income inequality the most dangerous part of what's going on in the United States."
– Alan Greenspan

If debt is a real issue and I for one don't think it is. And I'll tell you why; if you owned a billion dollars and planned to give it all to your family but squandered it off. Now you're broke so you fire up this machine you own called a mint or a moneymaking machine and you make another billion dollars. Who are you in debt to?

Yourself! Ok you're indebt to yourself, but you paid yourself back with your machine, what's your problem? There is none! It only exists in your thoughts. America owns that system, Greece doesn't. Because they didn't write it into their charter.

That's exactly what I'm talking about. If there is a debt due it is to the people. That's where we start our questioning. How can you send young men to wars to make fat cats millions when soldiers are getting blown up and coming home in pieces and get none of the billions Halliburton and the boys run off to buy new worlds.

November 26, 2014

I think most of us blacks agree with the no brainer of Michael Brown's wrongs for taking the cigarillos and walking in the street when told by the police to clear. My thoughts are, and I believe they are, what most blacks are trying to say. But before I continue let me preface that riots are the language spoken when no one is listening. American history was written from many of them, one being the Boston Tea Party! Us blacks see white men like James Holmes murder 12 people and wound 72 in a theater and yet be apprehended alive, we see fugitives like Eric Frein who ambushed and murdered Corporal Brian K Dicksen ll and the alleged tempted murder of trooper Alex Douglas, another state trooper in Pike County Pennsylvania be apprehended alive. We see Jared Loughner who shot and injured senator Gabby Gifford and murdered 12 people, apprehended alive. We can draw conclusions about Eric Harris and Dylan Klebold, the 16-year-old murderers of Columbine High School. When police arrived they never took a shot at them while the two continued to heinously murder 12 innocent young girls and boys. We can not draw a deduction as to why White America and its legal system imperatively will not allow Trayvon Martin and Michael Brown who did not kill anyone, live to have a fair trial, while almost always allowing these heinous murderers to be spared.

November 2014

In one year, the average American taxpayer making $50,000 a year pays:

$36 towards food stamps,

$6 for other safety net programs,

$870 for corporate subsidies,

$1600 to offset corporate tax loopholes,

and $1231 to offset losses from corporate overseas tax havens.

We can afford to help the poor, not corporate welfare.

(Sources: The Tax Foundation, Citizens for Tax Justice)

A big problem with this is that the people that need to read it will not! Because many Americans scream bloody murder over the 1-cent a day they pay towards welfare for the poor. While favoring to kiss the rich man's Ass at 10.2 cents a day which is $3,701 a year.

October 29, 2014

GAS PRICES ARE DOWN ALL OVER THE NATION, WITH THE EXCEPTION OF THE 20% CROOKS, THAT THINK IT AMERICAN TO CONTINUE GOUGING THE SHEEPLE IN THE NAME OF OBAMA! ANYONE BLAMING OBAMA FOR THE PRICE DECREASES YET?

2013

October 13, 2013

Give the country back to the Republicans forever and watch the earth and all that's in it degenerate, when there's no more EPA, unions, taxes, gun control, birth control, and let them maintain the only control they have now which is control of all the banks and what poor people can do and can't do. It will instantly become unfit for all except the uber rich!

October 11, 2013

If a person practices love toward all living people, animals and creatures, it doesn't make you anything but a loving, caring person. But if a person claims to be right (righteous), when in fact they are not, that individual is a hypocrite!

September 29, 2013

Politics defined, if you like it straight no chaser! When politics benefits the wealthy it's great, if it benefits the people it's bad; unfortunately most idiots on the wrong side, don't know any better!

September 29, 2013

There are some fundamental differences in the way Republican and Democratic politicians think. Here are just 12 examples:

1). Republicans fear that the government has too much control over corporations. Democrats fear that corporations have too much control over our government.

2). Democrats believe it benefits all of us to help the weakest and the poorest among us. Republicans believe it benefits all of us to help the wealthiest and most powerful among us.

3). Republicans believe large corporations will always do what is best for the American people if the government stays out of the way. Democrats believe large corporations would disembowel you and sell your organs to the highest bidder if the government didn't stop them.

4). Democrats believe everyone is entitled to health care regardless of their ability to pay. Republicans believe everyone is entitled to jack squat if they can't pay for health care.

5). Democrats believe too much of our money goes to crooked corporate executives who take government subsidies and pay themselves $80 million salaries. Republicans believe too much of our money goes to teachers who make $50,000 a year.

6). Democrats believe anything that helps the American people during a recession or a time of crisis is the true essence of patriotism. Republicans believe anything that helps the American people during a recession or a time of crisis is the true essence of communism.

7). Democrats believe that we need to set high standards for clean air and drinking water. Republicans believe that standards for clean air and water are burdensome over-regulation.

8). Democrats believe the President and Congress need to work together to create jobs during a weak economy. Republicans believe that Congress should do nothing to create jobs and then blame the President.

9). Democrats believe that corporate polluters should be made to pay for the cleanup of their pollution. Republicans believe that making corporations clean up their pollution is burdensome over-regulation.

10). Democrats believe our health care system exists solely for the purpose of making people healthy. Republicans believe our healthcare system exists solely for the purpose of making a healthy profit.

11). Democrats believe women should be the ones to decide what happens to their body. Republicans believe that men in the Catholic Church should make those decisions.

12). Democrats believe Congress should be of the people, by the people and for the people. Republicans believe corporations are the people.

September 9, 2013

Discussing religion, politics and health with most people, has a similar resemblance to, the legend of the Six Blind Men and the Elephant. There once were six blind men who, upon encountering an elephant, gave their own individual assessments of the elephant. The first one happened to fall against the broad and sturdy side of the elephant, and concluded that the elephant is very much like a wall. The second one, feeling the tusk, said the elephant was very much like a spear. The third one happened to take the squirming trunk in his hands, and said the elephant was very much like a snake. The fourth one, reached out and touched the elephant's knee, and concluded the elephant was very much like a tree. The fifth one happened to touch the ear, and insisted that the elephant is very much like a fan. And the sixth one seized the swinging tail, and said the elephant is very much like a rope. Each of the blind men was partly right based on his own subjective perception but at the same time, mostly wrong. The comical part of it all is that their dispute stemmed from utter ignorance because none had ever seen the elephant!

August 25, 2013

The Butler is the best movie I've ever seen on race, class and gender! I highly recommend watching it!

July 13, 2013

Had a gun-toting Trayvon Martin stalked an unarmed George Zimmerman, and then shot him to death... DO I EVEN NEED TO COMPLETE THIS SENTENCE?

July 13, 2013

Trayvon was black, and that made him wrong from the outset. I suppose he didn't have the right to wear a hoody, go to the store, or even visit his father's apartment. Justice for all is the same ole' injustice for us, it's scary out here guys. You never now what's next, I could tell you all a bunch of horror stories that would bedazzle you, but what good would it do? Nothing at all!

July 9, 2013

No one will ever know the exact details of what happened during the so called struggle, or if there really was a struggle. But logic that can only probe the walls that it cannot see beyond, can deduce the facts that we know and understand. We know that Trayvon was headed in the direction of his father's residence at the point of being pursued. We know that he was being stalked from his rear; we know that he was unarmed; we know that he has been called a thug and that no stolen goods were of his possession. We know that he was shot by the pursuer who was stalking him; we know that his pursuer had a gun, and we know that much hyperbole has been thrown at Trayvon Martin that is not necessarily true. But we do know that Zimmerman shot an unarmed 17-year-old boy. Those are the facts that we do know! My reasoning is this; Zimmerman had a job with much responsibility, perhaps to much for him in this case. I don't think Zimmerman should get life or a lot of time, I do believe he should receive 2 yrs. for exacerbating the situation!

April 26, 2013

(Genesis1: 6) And God said, let there be a firmament in the midst of the waters, and let it divide the waters from the waters. (Genesis1: 7) And God made the firmament, and divided the waters that were under the firmament from the waters that were above the firmament: and it was so. (Genesis1:8) And God called the firmament Heaven. Hence we walk around in Heaven every day!

April 26, 2013

I don't know why people would want to watch a station that just incites them. Do you want to be angry, paranoid and hateful all the time? Oh you do...well great, watch Fox "News". You'll be the most spiteful, angry person with the bonus of also being the least informed (studies have shown, that's not even snarky).

Let's take a look at the healing properties of coconut oil:

Coconut oil is antiviral, antifungal (kills yeast too) and antibacterial. It attacks and kills viruses that have a lipid (fatty) coating, such as herpes, HIV, hepatitis C, the flu, and mononucleosis. It kills the bacteria that cause pneumonia, sore throats, dental cavities, urinary tract infections, meningitis, gonorrhea, food poisoning, pneumonia, and many, many more bacterial infections. It kills the fungus/yeast infections that cause candida, ringworm, athlete's foot, thrush, jock itch, diaper rash and more.

Coconut oil is called the "low fat" fat. It actually acts like a carbohydrate in that it is quickly broken down in the liver and used as quick energy. It is NOT stored like other fats. It boosts one's energy and endurance. Many athletes use it blended into their drinks. It also supports thyroid function and increases your metabolism (great if you want to lose weight). Coconut oil improves digestion and absorption of fat-soluble vitamins, minerals (especially calcium and magnesium), and amino acids. It improves the body's use of blood glucose and improves insulin secretion and absorption (great for type II diabetes). In fact, many diabetics (type I and type II) use it to reduce their symptoms. One's risk of diabetes decreases with regular use of coconuts and coconut oil. And as we already mentioned, cooking with coconut oil does not create any harmful byproducts. Coconut oil helps the body heal and repair faster. It aids and supports immune function, protecting us from a variety of cancers. Coconut oil, contrary to much hubbub, is good for your heart. It keeps our blood platelets from sticking together (and causing dangerous clots). Regular users of coconut oils have a much lower chance of atherosclerosis (clogging of the arteries), arteriosclerosis (hardening of the arteries), and strokes. Coconut oil can lower your blood pressure. Coconut oil is a natural antioxidant. It protects the body from free radical damage and prevents premature aging and degenerative diseases.

Finally, coconut oil is the best massage oil on the planet. What it does to your skin, you simply have to witness. It forms a barrier against infections, softens and moisturizes your skin, and prevents wrinkling, sagging, and age spots. It promotes healthy hair and complexion, protects from any damaging UV rays.

March 17, 2013

(When I wrote this, I was actually reflecting on the Steubenville football players that were convicted of rape.) Without correct instructions and good family moral examples, most people, not all, gravitate to the lowest level of incompetence and error. Unfavorable examples for many children are too frequently abundant in today's society. Too many people teaching, preaching and thinking, that an absence or lack of discipline, equals love!

Like I said, Love is an action not a word! Also I mentioned that the law was fulfilled in scripture by love, yes God so loved the world that he gave... son, that if you believe in him you would have eternal life. That is the end time prophecy as well. Love cannot be used without meaning, love is meaning, without meaning its deception, a lie in other words.

March 7, 2013

In situations where only one parent is a United States citizen, he or she must have lived in the United States for at least five years at some point before the child's birth as a full American citizen, and at least two of these five years must have occurred after the parent's 14th birthday. In the case of a child born to an American mother, the child is usually considered a citizen, whether or not the mother is married. If an American father is involved in a relationship with a foreign woman and the couple is not married, however, the father may need to fight for the child's right to citizenship.

February 19, 2013

Regarding Oscar winning actor Forrest Whitaker being falsely accused of shoplifting from a New York deli… "Blacks have had to endure these insults since time immemorial, the sad part is that the jerks who are actually guilty of shoplifting, or other crimes often go un-accused because many people are afraid to approach them."

January 8, 2013

Chicago banned guns yet still has a gun problem? Why? Study of guns used in Chicago crimes found most came from just a few gun stores who illegally sold them; gun stores located 200-300 miles away from Chicago! ((Evidence of why we'd need a national gun law, now local gun laws, before we'd see a decline in gun crimes)) Bloomberg in NYC had the NYPD trace back the source of guns used in violent crime in NYC a couple years back. Turned out literally 60% of all gun-related crimes involved guns purchased from just six gun stores found in VA and SC! Attempts to hold those stores responsible for illegal gun sales, however, failed.

January 4, 2013

The GOP as far back as before the Great Depression, has been lying to the American people and using scare tactics about the National Debt. They make false statements claiming that our grandchildren will be strapped with paying the debt created in our time. This is a totally false statement because our current National Debt is not the largest that it has ever been. There really is no desperate (or any, for that matter) need to reduce the debt. The debt is not nearly as big as some lead people to believe. The deception can be found in how it is measured; in dollar terms it is the largest ever. But you could say that about everything in reference to the cost of things, compared to that of the 60's. Grocery bills, house payments, a new car, etc.

For example, a $26,000 car would cost $2,600 in the 60's, that's 10 times more. Have things become 10 times better? Of course not. The average income has increased by 10 times; a $50,000 salary would be $5,000 in the 60's. So in this light, the National Debt is the biggest ever. Unlike Greece, America is denominated in it's own currency and cannot be forced to default on debt. The American government is designed in a way that its federal government debt is not analogous to that in the private sector because it represents an injection of wealth, not a drag on growth. In other words it owns the ability to print money in order to bail out or stimulate growth.

January 2, 2013

"It is incumbent on every generation to pay its own debts as it goes. A principle which if acted on would save one-half the wars of the world."- Thomas Jefferson

2012

December 20, 2012

For all you that believe the world is going to end tonight, leave me your bank account info, your mortgage papers, your car's pink slip and all your valuable possessions and I will keep and take great care of them for you!

December 18, 2012

America needs to work on reducing their many forms of violence. From the top down, this country has been, and is a killing machine. Most of the children here don't have a chance, violence is sold on video games, TV commercials, movies, even the news, rap and rock music, etc. It's a moral condition and guns are another form of fuel that feeds the fire. Advocating guns as a solution to the violence is like extinguishing a fire with gasoline.

November 8, 2012

And the entire congregation lifted up their voice, and cried; and the people wept that night. (Numbers 14:2) And wherefore hath the Lord brought us unto this land, to fall by the sword, that our wives and children should be a prey? Were it not better for us to return into Egypt? (Numbers 14:3) And they said one to another, Let us make a captain, and let us return into Egypt? (Numbers 14:4) Only rebel not against the Lord, neither fear ye the people of the land; for they (are) bread for us. (Numbers 14:9) And the Lord said unto Moses, How long will these people provoke me? And how long will it be ere they believe me, for all the signs which I have showed among them? (Numbers 14:11) I will smite them with pestilence, and disinherit them, and will make of thee a greater nation and mightier than they. (Numbers 14:12) In the above text the Israelites murmured against their gracious and loving God. Needless to say, their murmurings displeased Him. Sadly, many Christians are murmurers and complainers. In the home, on the job and in the local church they grumble, murmur and complain. They can see nothing good. To them, everything is bad -- their life is miserable and they want to make it that way for everyone else. To murmur means to grumble or whine. It is not wrong to complain if correction is needed, but there should be no murmuring.

November 7, 2012

Last night hatred, racism, Fox News, and Limbaugh lost. Compassion, humanity and the American people won. Now Mr. Boehner you guys in Congress start doing something for the American People and stop using all your efforts fighting against our President. You work for us, and as of last night we the people that you WORK FOR have told you our choice. Live with it and move on. We need a Congress that works with the President not against him. Get to work.

November 2, 2012

This is all the GOP has so Fox News keeps talking about it. Last night I thought, "I wonder if Fox is still trying to use this" so I changed the station. I kid you not; the first WORD I heard as soon as I turned the station to Fox was "Benghazi."

What all of the Righties are conveniently forgetting is the following: Obama tried to get MORE security and was DENIED BY THE REPUBLICANS in congress. The republicans reduced the security budget for these embassies by almost half a billion dollars in 2011 and 2012. Hillary

Clinton warned it was a big mistake for the Republicans to take funding away and to deny beefing up security and look what happens. Of course the Republicans, ever the finger pointers, refuse to be held accountable and are instead blaming Obama for their actions. Also, don't forget the SEVEN embassy attacks in the Middle East under Bush, which resulted in 20 deaths and many injuries.

2002: U.S. Consulate In Karachi, Pakistan, Attacked; 10 Killed, 51 Injured.

2004: U.S. Embassy Bombed In Uzbekistan.

2004: Gunmen Stormed U.S. Consulate In Saudi Arabia.

2006: Armed Men Attacked U.S. Embassy In Syria.

2007: Grenade Launched Into U.S. Embassy In Athens.

2008: Rioters Set Fire To U.S. Embassy In Serbia.

2008: Ten People Killed In Bombings At U.S. Embassy In Yemen.

This is just about Embassies though. If we go back to Clinton's administration there was a time when Clinton had an opportunity to take Bin Laden out. The republicans in Congress all shot that request down and instead focused on more "important" things like going after Clinton for messing around on the side with Lewinski. Fast forward to 9/11/01 and we have over 3,000 men, women and children murdered because Bin Laden wasn't taken care of when we had the chance and Clinton wanted to. Then of course there's also the warming Bush had 2 months before the attacks.

October 25, 2012

Obama inherits a nearly 10 trillion-dollar deficit and two ongoing costly wars from George Bush. The U.S. faces economic meltdown at home, throwing the country into a 1930s

Depression-like crisis. He tries to deliver despite obstructionism by the other side. Republicans question his citizenship, his name, his religion and his agenda. They call him a socialist, a Muslim and a weak leader. He tries to be polite, civil, and works hard to reach out to the other side. They reject him. They use every means to undermine him, viciously and mercilessly.

October 25, 2012

Why I will vote for Obama! The cause of the recent spike in national debt is obvious, the Afghanistan and Iraq wars under George Bush, the housing bubble that both sides don't claim, the bailout package under both parties, and the economic stimulus package by Barack Obama, are main factors in causing this increase in the debt. Barack Obama is asking that the debt ceiling be raised so that America does not default on it's loans and cause a crisis. Republicans on the other hand are demanding that the ceiling not be raised; they believe that government spending any money is completely wrong. Christine Lagarde, the acting head of the International Monetary Fund, has publicly stated that the situation needs to be resolved immediately with responsible financial policies. There is no doubt that these financial policies are deliberate, and a targeted, planned destruction of the living standards of working class Americans. This is clearly intended to cut the healthcare and education of the American masses. Essentially, the people of America are going to have to pay for the actions of the ruling elite.

Unfortunately, even though this is a very serious situation with serious repercussions for the entire world, both sides, Democrats and Republicans, have used this incident for political point scoring and for standing on soap boxes, rather than coming together and dealing with this emergency. Even US Federal Reserve chairman Ben Bernaki has come out and said this is a dangerous game to be playing and there needs to be bipartisanship to take care of this problem.

Political point scoring is not a good idea right now - there needs to be a bipartisan campaign to end this problem before it gets worse.

In a situation like this we can see the short-sidedness of the bourgeoisie. They are putting all this effort into gaining whatever they can for themselves, rather than dealing with a major problem that's coming up ahead that could crash the entire economy. Immediate profit is more important than the future stability of the system that they believe in. Republicans have been fighting the idea of the debt ceiling being raised. Instead, they demand that there should be austerity measures; cutting healthcare and education of the average working American and making them suffer for what the ruling elite has done. Now, despite their adamant stance against the raising of the debt ceiling, they themselves have been pretty big supporters of raising the debt ceiling in the past. Since 1962 the debt ceiling has been raised 74 times; 18 times under Ronald Reagan, 7 times under George W. Bush.

This debt ceiling raising has a very big history with the Republican Party, despite their adamant stance against it right now. The only solution seems to be (within the framework of capitalism itself) is to raise the debt ceiling a little bit enough to get things going and to not allow a default to happen. Then there would come the immediate ceasing of all the wars (Afghanistan, Iraq, Pakistan, and Libya) - end all military conquest. More than 60% of the US national budgetis spent on national defense. Ending most military spending and cutting it down to 20% of the national budget would free up a ton of money, allowing the debt to be paid down very quickly. The lack of wars in the last ten years would have put a

serious dent into the debt crisis. But again, if those wars hadn't have happened, we wouldn't be in the situation that we are in! Lastly, increase taxes on the top 10%-20% of Americans; the US has the second lowest corporate tax rate in the world.

Increasing taxes on the elite would certainly help pay for a debt that they had a huge hand in creating.

October 21, 2012

"Deep in the heart of man, there are two contradictory loves, neither of which can ever blossom fully except at the expense of the other; the love of self, which can grow until it becomes the scorn of God; the love of God, which must grow until it becomes the scorn of self. The former-of which the love of the "world" or the love of creatures are only variants, and for which concupiscence is the theological name and self-love the profane equivalent-is the result of the corruption provoked by original sin. It is a deviation of the one true love that leads man towards his natural end, God. Man, given over to his own devices, in the fallen condition to which sin has reduced him, never acts except for love of self. He can do good only when guided by the love of God, also called "charity," which only grace can inspire in him. Thus the passage from love of self to love of God constitutes the fundamental religious act that is called, in spiritual language, "conversion". ---Pascal

October 21, 2012

In the first year of Obama's administration the world gave him the Nobel Peace Prize because they were sick of Republican preemptive war shoot-em up cowboy policies. Romney has already got the rest of the world angry by his aggressive warmonger Bush-like talk. Now, you have countries that think they will be in his cross hairs preparing to defend themselves or even worse. George Bush and Cheney used peace through strength as an excuse to attack Iraq over made up WMD claims. This is the problem with a preemptive war or first strike policy. Reagan built up the military but never promoted a first strike or preemptive war policy. But the Republican Party through Bush and Cheney thinks a preemptive war policy is a good thing. Romney is supporting a strike on Iran and his statements toward Russia, China, Syria, Afghanistan and Iraq are of the highest concern. We must not support a party that supports preemptive war, which is dangerous in the nuclear age. Obama is a peacemaker and has ended the preemptive war in Iraq and is seeking a peaceful solution to Iran's nuclear ambitions and ways to work out a deal with the Russians over their concerns. Under the leadership of Putin, Russia has recently launched all three components of a nuclear triad, land and sea long-range nuclear missiles, and bombs in a test involving command systems. This was the most comprehensive test by the Russians since the 1991 collapse. Do we need jobs at the expense of great nuclear wars?

October 3, 2012

You have to love Mitt Romney's Plan for the Nation as President, To mention a thousand times what Obama has or has not done! While not revealing a plan of his own, outside of repeating the same thing that got us here!

September 23, 2012

People should be ashamed telling God in a prayer that there are more of them that believe. Do you think God is stupid and can't do his own math? Things are getting worse because the salt has lost its savor and that's a reflection on the believer not the nonbeliever. God fills the entire volume of the universe; you can't take him out of anything. He lives in the heart and not in the word. Besides scripture says the hypocrite likes to pray outwardly to be seen of man and that you should pray in your closet, stop lying to God and expecting blessings. God's blessings are everlasting and continual and he blesses the unjust as he does the just!

August 15, 2012

On Tim Tebow's Decision to Pose Shirtless for GQ Magazine:

It might do Tebow some good to review what Jesus says in the book of Matthews 6:5-6 about wanting to be seen of men. In fact a lot of misinformed want to be Christians should read it!

August 1, 2012

"We have deluded ourselves into believing the myth that capitalism grew and prospered out of the Protestant work ethic of hard work and sacrifices. Capitalism was built on the exploitation of black slaves and continues to thrive on the exploitation of the poor, both black and white, both here and abroad." - Dr. Martin Luther King, Jr. –

July 7, 2012

CONTAMINATION OF THE FOOD CHAIN

The National Academy of Sciences recently estimated that 15% of the American people are presently afflicted with allergies to one or more chemical products. The study pointed out that we are exposed to more toxic chemicals while inside our homes than when we go out. The chemicals which are found in every home include benzene, which causes Leukemia; the common moth spray and mothballs containing para-dichlorobenzene, whose use forms an invisible but damaging gas in some thirty million American homes; Lindane, a common pesticide; chlordane, used for termite control (chlordane has been much in the news lately because of some families who became deathly ill after their homes has been treated by professional termite exterminators; one couple had to move out and totally abandon their home, after inspectors informed them there was no way it could be sufficiently cleansed of the chlordane residues to be habitable). Chloroform compounds are much more common in homes than is popularly realized. The EPA has found that chloroform levels inside of homes were five times greater than outside. Persons taking hot shower baths inside a closed curtain are unaware that they are inhaling substantial amounts of chloroform from the steam (if not using well water). Heating the water releases the chlorine in the heavily chlorinated water, which then emerges as a gas while the hot water comes from the nozzle. A daily shower is guaranteed to give you chloroform high. Formaldehyde is also present in many homes in a number of commonly used compounds. The daily ingestion of minute portions of any or all of these household chemicals contributes to the development of cancers, as they are sufficiently toxic to become carcinogenic in daily contact.

July 6, 2012

When the Bush administration turned Clinton's peace, prosperity and surpluses into the exact opposite, culminating in the bursting of the housing bubble, the mortgage mess, the Great Recession and the financial crisis, the GOP had a decision to make as to how they were going to handle this politically. Running up the debt and ruining the economy was not exactly something to run on, so what did they do? They created an alternate reality.

In this false version of reality, Obama created the huge deficits, not the Bush administration. Obama was said to have made the economy worse, contrary to economic statistics. The debt-ceiling crisis caused by the GOP, and the resulting S&P downgrade, was twisted into being the

"Obama downgrade." The GOP's "government should get out

of the way" ideology allowed the financial sector to self-destruct, but this was turned into

"government forced the banks to make bad loans" by right-wing propagandists. And so forth.

The Republican Party made a cynical and deliberate decision to lie, distort and obstruct in order

to preserve and enhance their political standing. Too many people have been hoodwinked by

their rhetoric or have simply failed to be vigilant, so they've gotten away with murder. While the

GOP continues to talk down the economy and undermine almost anything designed to put the

American economy on better footing, the public continues to be complacent or ignorant about

what's been going on. I've never seen anything quite like it.

June 30, 2012

Why I like Obama-care!

Insurance companies no longer have unchecked power to cancel your policy, deny your child

coverage due to a pre-existing condition, or charge women more than men. Over 86 million

Americans have gained from coverage of preventive care free of charge, like mammograms for

women and wellness visits for seniors. Nearly 13 million Americans will receive a rebate this

summer because their insurance company spent too much of their premium dollars on

administrative costs or CEO bonuses.

The law has already helped 5.3 million seniors and people with disabilities save an average of

over $600 on prescription drugs in the "donut hole" in Medicare coverage. The law's provisions

to strengthen and protect Medicare by fighting fraud will continue. The law has helped 6.6

million young adults who have been able to stay on their parents' plans until the age of 26, including 3.1 million young people who are newly insured.

June 17, 2012

"Before you speak to me about your religion, first show it to me in how you treat other people; Before you tell me how much you love your God, show me how you love all his children; Before you preach to me of your passion for your faith, teach me about it through your compassion for your neighbor. In the end, I'm not as interested in what you have to tell or sell as in how you choose to live and give."

-Cory Booker, Mayor of Newark, New Jersey

March 7, 2012

When the Bush administration turned Clinton's peace, prosperity and surpluses into the exact opposite, culminating in the bursting of the housing bubble, the mortgage mess, the Great Recession and the financial crisis, the GOP had a decision to make as to how they were going to handle this politically. Running up the debt and ruining the economy was not exactly something to run on, so what did they do? They created an alternate reality.

In this false version of reality, Obama created the huge deficits, not the Bush administration. Obama was said to have made the economy worse, contrary to economic statistics. The debt-ceiling crisis caused by the GOP, and the resulting S&P downgrade, was twisted into being the "Obama downgrade." The GOP's "government should get out of the way" ideology allowed the financial sector to self-destruct, but this was turned into "government forced the banks to make bad loans" by right-wing propagandists. And so forth.

The Republican Party made a cynical and deliberate decision to lie, distort and obstruct in order to preserve and enhance their political standing. Too many people have been hoodwinked by their rhetoric or have simply failed to be vigilant, so they've gotten away with murder. While the GOP continues to talk down the economy and undermine almost anything designed to put the American economy on better footing, the public continues to be complacent or ignorant about what's been going on. I've never seen anything quite like it.

January 29, 2012

I think Obama's biggest problem is the racism our Great Americans (GOP) are so relentlessly willing to share. I say that because Ronald Reagan whose style was very similar, is revered as a Republican all time favorite.

1). Reagan was notorious for raising taxes.

2). Reagan grew the size of the Federal government tremendously.

3). Reagan nearly tripled the Federal budget.

4). Unemployment soared after 1981 tax cuts.

5). Reagan illegally funneled weapons to Iran.

6). Reagan helped to create the Taliban and Osama Bin Laden.

7). Reagan gave amnesty to 3 million undocumented immigrants.

8). Reagan vetoed a comprehensive Anti-Apartheid Act, which placed sanctions on South Africa and cut of all American trade with the country. The Republican controlled Senate overrode Reagan's veto.

January 5, 2012

The worsening of the economy in the years before the stock market crash is troubling for conservative defenders of the Roaring Twenties. The economic policies were strictly Republican; there was no Big Government to blame for the onset of the Depression. Money was based on the gold standard, yet another pet conservative ideology. The tax burden was the lightest since World War I to this day. Yet even before October 29, 1929, it was clear that the economy was in trouble and that things were only going to get worse.

January 3, 2012

The State of Iowa should be the poster child for the Obama Campaign. "Iowa, one of several Midwestern states that largely sidestepped the reckless rise of the housing market and the crash that followed, has remained relatively stable through these difficult years. Buoyed by a booming agriculture sector, the state is enjoying lower unemployment, greater income growth, steadier home sales and fewer foreclosures than most others". (NY Times 12/17/11)

Additionally, they are the recipients of US Government welfare/stimulus programs; only in Iowa it's called Farm Subsidies. In fact, in 2010 they received $1,332,867,836 or $454 per person, compared to the amount of welfare/stimulus payments in the State of Massachusetts, $1,700,000,000 or $260 per person, about half of what Iowans receive. While Iowa demonstrates how well stimulus works, it's interesting to see how they resist using it for others.

2011

Lets see if I got this correctly. Obama inherited all of Iraq, and Afghanistan war, high unemployment, housing market crash, and stock market at 8. And carmakers filing for bankruptcy.

Accomplishments: Ended the Iraq war by getting out so we don't keep killing our servicemen, and stop wasting tax dollars. Eventually got Mubarak out of his regime, Gadhafi is gone, took out Bin Laden thanks to "Seal Team 6", G.M is paying back the money loaned and saved a lot of workers from being laid off, (and as I hear it this morning has now over taken Toyota as the #1 car maker) stock market at 8, received a Nobel Peace Prize, and the unemployment rate is slowly dropping. All this in 3 years. Compared to the prior administration taking eight years to undo all the good that was left him.

October 2, 2011

Know the truth about the lie's Limbaugh, Hannity, Levine, Barks, and Daniels tell you about Fannie Mae and Freddie Mac loans and how they blame Barney Frank!